Eastern Europe

Jennifer Prior, Ph.D.

Consultants

William O'Mara, Ph.D.
History Professor
California State University, Dominguez Hills

Jon Anger
English, History, and ELD Teacher
Novato Unified School District

Publishing Credits

Rachelle Cracchiolo, M.S.Ed., *Publisher*
Emily R. Smith, M.A.Ed., *SVP of Content Development*
Véronique Bos, *Vice President of Creative*
Dani Neiley, *Editor*
Fabiola Sepulveda, *Series Graphic Designer*

Image Credits: p.6 (top) Shutterstock/Teimy Photos; p.6 (bottom) Shutterstock/Aljohara Jewel; p.11 Alamy/image broker; p.12 (top) Wikimedia; p.13 (top) Shutterstock/Footage Clips; p.13 (bottom) Alamy/Imaginechina Limited; p.14 Alamy/Pluto; p.15 (top) Alamy/Cum Okolo; p.17 (top) Shutterstock/Serhii Shcherbyna; p.17 (bottom) Library of Congress [LC-DIG-ppmsc-03931]; p.18 Shutterstock/Banifacyj; p.19 Alamy/CTK; p.20 Alamy/Nataliya Yurchenko; p.21 Shutterstock/Ventura; p.22 (top) Alamy/Shawshots; p.22 (bottom) Alamy/Superstock; p.24 Shutterstock/Aleksandr Sosnin; p.27 (top) Shutterstock/Afinn Stock; p.32 Shutterstock/Ducu Rodionoff; all other images from iStock and/or Shutterstock

Library of Congress Cataloging-in-Publication Data

Names: Prior, Jennifer Overend, 1963- author.
Title: Eastern Europe / Jennifer Prior, PhD.
Description: Huntington Beach, CA : Teacher Created Materials, Inc, [2023] | Includes index. | Audience: Ages 8-18 | Summary: "The people of eastern Europe are as diverse as the region. The land varies from mild, coastal climates to the subarctic. The people have rich traditions. They take pride in their cultures. And, they face challenges with great strength. Let's get to know this unique and resolute region!"-- Provided by publisher.
Identifiers: LCCN 2022038214 (print) | LCCN 2022038215 (ebook) | ISBN 9781087695136 (paperback) | ISBN 9781087695297 (ebook)
Subjects: LCSH: Europe, Eastern--Juvenile literature.
Classification: LCC DJK39.5 .P75 2023 (print) | LCC DJK39.5 (ebook) | DDC 947--dc23/eng/20220810
LC record available at https://lccn.loc.gov/2022038214
LC ebook record available at https://lccn.loc.gov/2022038215

DECEBALUS REX
DRAGAN FECIT

Shown on the cover is Prague, Czechia.

TCM | Teacher Created Materials

5482 Argosy Avenue
Huntington Beach, CA 92649
www.tcmpub.com
ISBN 978-1-0876-9513-6
© 2023 Teacher Created Materials, Inc.

Table of Contents

Rich Heritage. 4

The Lay of the Land 6

The European Divide. 10

Indigenous Peoples 12

Today's Culture. 14

Let's Talk Civics. 18

Economics through Time. 22

Proud and Resolute. .26

Map It! 28

Glossary 30

Index 31

Learn More!. 32

Danube River in Romania

Rich Heritage

Eastern Europe lies between western Europe and Asia. The land includes **coastal** regions and mountains. It has areas of tundra and the subarctic.

This region is home to many people and cultures. Every country in eastern Europe has distinct ways of life. Meaningful traditions are a part of each one. The people there have a rich and proud heritage.

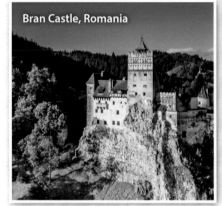
Bran Castle, Romania

The people of eastern Europe have faced considerable challenges. This region has seen a lot of war. But the people persisted through hardships. They are **resilient**. Many are standing up to those who want to keep them **oppressed**.

Eastern Europe continues to grow and change. Let's get to know this diverse and **resolute** region.

RUSSIA
Europe

RUSSIA
Asia

The Lay of the Land

Europe is the second-smallest continent. It is often grouped by four regions: eastern, western, southern, and northern. All the countries of Europe are west of Asia. Several eastern European countries are bordered by bodies of water. Russia is the largest country in this region.

winter in Kaliningrad, Russia

winter in Evia, Greece

Carpathian Mountains

Climate

This region consists of coastal areas, plains, forests, and mountains. These areas, along with **latitude** and **elevation**, greatly affect the climate. Most of eastern Europe has cold winters. Closer to the southern coast, the climate is much milder. There is little frost in the winter. This is true for Greece, Albania, and Montenegro. In contrast, the Russian north is quite different. It has a subarctic climate. Winters in this region are long and cold. Parts of Finland also have hard winters.

Carpathian Mountains

The Carpathian Mountains span many of the eastern European countries. This includes Serbia and Romania. The foothills have a mild climate. The alpine zone is higher in elevation. It is much colder and has snow for more than seven months out of the year.

A Mountainous Border

The Ural Mountains run through Russia. Remember how Russia spans two continents? The Urals separate Europe and Asia. This narrow mountain range serves as a natural boundary between the two continents. It is around 1,550 miles (2,500 kilometers) long.

Seas and Waterways

Many of the countries in eastern Europe are bordered by bodies of water. These include the Baltic Sea, the Adriatic Sea, the Black Sea, and the Caspian Sea. However, some countries in this region are landlocked, such as North Macedonia and Kosovo. That means there are no large bodies of water along their borders. This region also has many rivers that are passable by large boats.

The Danube River

The Danube is the second-longest river in Europe. It passes through 10 countries. Eight of these are in eastern Europe. The river begins in the Black Forest mountains of Germany. It flows for more than 1,777 miles (2,860 kilometers) and empties into the Black Sea. Hundreds of years ago, the Danube served as a boundary between **empires**. Today, it serves as access for trade. The Danube has more than 300 **tributaries**. Thirty of these are passable by boat.

Danube River in Budapest, Hungary

The Danube River merges with the Black Sea in Romania.

The Black Sea

The Black Sea serves as a transportation route among countries. It is a saltwater sea that is home to 180 different kinds of fish. Fishing in the Black Sea has provided many resources for people in that area. The six countries that border the sea work to protect it. For example, the hunting of bottlenose dolphins is now banned in the Black Sea.

Hydroelectric Power

Did you know that water can create electricity? Fast flowing water moves with great force. It can spin a **turbine**. The turbine **generates** electric power as it spins. Many countries along the Danube depend on this hydroelectric power. Other European countries also depend on this power. Turkey, Italy, Portugal, and Spain are a few.

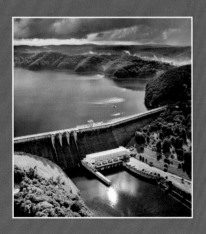

The European Divide

The Soviet Union played a large role in eastern Europe's history. It was formed in 1922. The Soviet Union became one of the most powerful countries in the world. It was made of 15 separate republics. Russia was the largest. Some eastern European countries in the union included Belarus and Ukraine. The union was ruled by the Communist Party. Some countries that were in the Soviet Union did not want to be part of it. But for years, they remained under communist rule. During that time, the Soviet Union had control over them.

After the end of World War II, another war developed. This was called the *Cold War*. People did not fight in battles. But there was a lot of tension among countries. There was a divide between Eastern and Western Europe. This divide was known as the "Iron Curtain." The "curtain" was imaginary. It separated Europe into two sections.

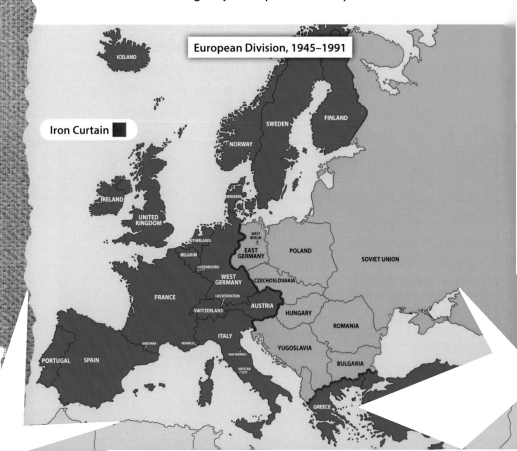

European Division, 1945–1991

Iron Curtain

Eastern European countries were under Soviet influence. The Soviet Union wanted people in those countries to stay away from other countries. The Soviets did not want their people to be influenced by areas that were not communist.

In 1991, the Soviet Union broke up. The combined country split into individual countries once again. This marked a new chapter for countries in eastern Europe. Optimism spread through the region. Many countries elected new leadership. They began to rebuild toward a freer future.

What Is Communism?

Communism is a political and economic system. In communist theory, wealth is meant to be shared. People cannot own anything that helps them make goods. People work according to their abilities. Goods are distributed according to people's needs. The ultimate goal is to have a classless society. This is meant to be fair for everyone.

Sami people in the early 1900s

Indigenous Peoples

There are a number of **Indigenous** groups in eastern Europe. Many people have lived on the land for thousands of years.

The Sami

The Sami people are likely the oldest native Europeans to still live in tribes. The **ancestors** of the Sami first came to northern **Scandinavia**. Some historians think Sami history can be traced back thousands of years.

The Sami hunted and herded reindeer. They lived life as **nomads**. This means they moved from place to place. Groups of five or six families hunted together. They also fished for food. Their homes were tents or huts with turf roofs. This made it look like the roofs of the houses were covered in grass.

a Sami house in Norway

This man wears traditional Sami clothes in Finland.

The Sami still live in Scandinavia. Some of them also live on the Kola Peninsula in Russia. There are now about 70,000 Sami people. The Sami do not move around much compared to the past. Many families live in houses. One member of each family is in charge of herding their reindeer.

Like other Indigenous groups, the Sami face some unfair treatment from others. They worry about the takeover of their land. Companies have been interested in the natural resources that can be found on Sami land. But the Sami need the land for their animals to graze.

Joik

Joik (YOY-keh) is a way for Sami people to express themselves through music. Joik is often a mixture of chanting with melodies. Some Sami individuals have their own joik. It is a musical representation of who they are.

Today's Culture

Every country in this region is unique. Each one has a culture of its own. Let's learn about some of them.

Belarus

The people of Belarus love the arts. They are well-known for their music, dance, art, and literature. Belarus hosts two yearly international festivals for art and music. Throughout the country, people like to eat locally grown crops. Potatoes are served in many different dishes. This includes potato and onion pancakes called *draniki*.

Bulgaria

One tradition in Bulgaria is **Thracian** fire dancing. People dance barefoot on top of hot coals. Fire dancing involves quick steps so the dancers don't get burned. It requires skill and should not be tried at home! Festivals are another popular tradition in Bulgaria. There is an international **folklore** festival each year. At this festival, people share their folk songs and dances.

Czechia

The Czech Republic is also known as Czechia. Czech people enjoy many outdoor sports. In the summer, they like to golf, ride bikes, and hike. In the winter, snowboarding, skiing, and hockey are popular.

Czech people also created the polka dance. This quick, lively dance is popular across the world. Dancers rotate in circles using half-steps.

traditionally dressed polka dancers

Moldova

At one point, Moldova was part of Romania. For that reason, the two cultures share the same language and folk traditions. Football (also known as soccer) is a beloved sport here. Every year, teams compete for the Moldovan Cup. It's a national competition.

Romania

Romanian culture is known for its folk art. People make wood carvings, woven rugs, and pottery. Painted Easter eggs are popular in this country. It is common to see religious icons in Romanian art.

Lithuania

Folk art is popular in Lithuania. Paper cutting is one type of folk art. This involves cutting elaborate designs out of colored paper. In the past, this type of art was used as decoration. Today, it is used frequently on greeting cards. Knitting and designing dyed Easter eggs are also popular types of folk art.

Poland

Polish people take great pride in their music. Musical events and festivals are common across the country. Many Polish people are fans of classical music. Polish jazz is known worldwide for its creativity.

Family members are often close with one another in Poland. Three generations sometimes live together. So, children, parents, and grandparents may share homes.

Russia

Russia is also known as the Russian Federation. It is the largest country in the world and has a mix of cultures. There are more than 120 different ethnic groups. More than 100 languages are spoken in Russia. Ethnic Russians make up four-fifths of Russia's population. They are known for their hospitality. They are welcoming and love to have guests.

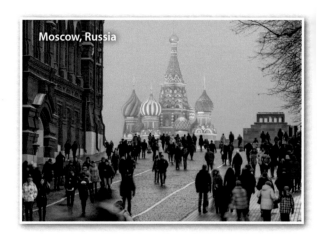
Moscow, Russia

Slovakia

The culture of Slovakia has many influences. The surrounding countries of Austria, Hungary, and Germany affect Slovakia's culture. Some food and drink in Slovakia has been influenced by these cultures.

The people of Slovakia value stories from their past. Artistic drawings of these stories can be seen in Catholic churches. Many of their traditions are religious in nature.

Ukraine

Ukrainian culture has been influenced in some ways by Polish culture. Ukrainians love traditions. Some people love to serve traditional food dishes. One popular dish is *borscht*. This is a

dancers in Ukraine

beet soup eaten either hot or cold. This dish is popular across eastern Europe. But the people in each country may have slight adjustments to the dish. For example, the Ukrainian version includes more ingredients than the Lithuanian version.

The Nenets

The Nenets are an Indigenous group. They live in Russia. They believe in many spirits who guide their lives. The Nenets are nomads. They follow reindeer as they migrate. They make warm coats, gloves, hoods, and boots from reindeer fur.

Let's Talk Civics

Governments in each of the eastern European countries are different. Some of them are republics. In a republic, power is held by the people. They elect people to represent them. Each eastern European republic has an elected president.

Civic engagement is low in some parts of the region. This dates back to the fall of communism. People struggled to trust those in power. But, more people are starting to get involved.

Belarus

A new constitution of Belarus was written in 1994. In 1996, the government changed it to increase the powers given to the president. As of 2022, there has only been one president of Belarus. Civic engagement in this country is low. It is believed that elections are often not fair. Many young people are trying to change things. They want freedom and rights. They want to express themselves freely. They want freedom from oppression.

People in Belarus protest against the president.

Czechia

In Czechia, there is a president and a prime minister. The people vote to elect these leaders. Lawmakers work in a group called *Parliament*. It is split into two parts. The first part is the Senate. The second part is the Chamber of Deputies. People in Czechia engage with their government by voting. And in recent years, many people in Czechia have been volunteering their time in their communities. Some lead hobby activities and do tasks to help people.

The former prime minister of Czechia launches his campaign.

Hungary

Hungarians are looking for ways to create change in their communities. One organization is working with the Hungarian youth. Their goal is to help young people engage more with their communities.

Accountability

Accountability can be part of civic engagement. It means to hold people responsible for their actions. In Hungary, a nonprofit group provides data to the public. They document and challenge their government's spending decisions. They want to prevent corruption. Keeping the public aware of what's going on in the government is their main goal.

Moldova

People in Moldova are becoming more active in their governments. Many people took part in a community program across the country. They learned about their local governments. Some people looked at how money was spent in their cities.

Poland

Civic engagement in Poland is on the rise. They have had higher engagement compared to other places in this region. Some Polish people join parent groups. Others join volunteer fire departments. People find all kinds of ways to get involved.

anti-war meeting in Warsaw, Poland

Romania

Young people are leading the way in Romania. Recently, young people have been taking action with government issues. They want to change political and economic **corruption**.

Russia

In Russia, the most involved citizens are young. Many are under the age of 30. They have college educations. They are often middle class. And they use social media a lot. But it can be dangerous for them to speak out against the government. Some of them face consequences. This may include fines or prison time.

Slovakia

In Slovakia, people in power are viewed poorly. They are seen as people who break promises. This affects civic engagement. Many young people protest to make their voices heard and change that view.

anti-government protest in Slovakia

Ukraine

Ukrainians are proud of their country. They take great pride in their culture. In 2022, Russia invaded Ukraine. Many people died. But Ukrainians never stopped fighting, determined to **safeguard** their people and their heritage.

Making a Difference

Rita Naumenko is a 16-year-old activist in Russia. She is hoping to stop climate change. At a protest, she held a handmade sign. Translated, it says that "The Earth Is Everybody's Responsibility."

Земля касается каждого

Economics through Time

People celebrated the end of World War II in 1945. But the war's end brought new challenges for many countries. Some of the most affected countries were in Eastern Europe.

People were forced to flee when their towns were destroyed.

The war caused many economic challenges for eastern Europe. Countries had to use a lot of their resources for the war efforts. During the war, many towns were destroyed. This caused many countries to lose resources and money. And many eastern Europeans died in the war. An important workforce of young men lost their lives.

Eastern European countries struggled to build back. It was a slow process to rebuild everything. Still, the economies of the region have improved over time. A lot of progress has been made since the end of the Soviet Union.

Cologne, Germany, after World War II

Present-Day Economies

Some eastern European economies are thriving today. Czechia, Slovakia, and Estonia are listed among the most advanced **economies** in the world. Poland, Romania, and Latvia are listed as growing economies. There has been an increase in economic success. This is because the region has a high number of people who are educated. Many people speak more than one language. These are great advantages in business.

The countries in this region are known for making goods. The region is also known for farming and fishing. It uses its many seas and waterways to distribute goods to other countries.

Czech Language

The Czech language is not very common. It is also a difficult one to learn for English speakers. Interestingly enough, one Czech word is very familiar in English. The word *robot* exists thanks to a Czech writer. Karel Čapek used the word *robot* in his play after his brother, Josef, suggested it.

Industries

Several eastern European countries make cars. Škoda is a car made in Czechia. Slovakia makes cars for Kia. Hungary produces cars for Mercedes-Benz. Some Ford cars are made in Romania. People around the world depend on cars made in this region.

paper factory in Russia

Eastern European countries make more than cars. Tools are made in Bulgaria and Romania. Bulgaria and Czechia make military hardware. Factories in Russia make paper. Clothing and textiles are made in Moldova, Bulgaria, and other countries in the region. Thousands of people work in factories making clothing.

Russia has a massive supply of oil and gas. This is due to the country's large size. Oil is Russia's biggest export. Russia moves oil to other countries through pipelines. Ships also carry Russia's oil around the world.

Technology is another big industry in the region. Czechia, Poland, and Hungary make electronics. Belarus builds machines. These goods are exported all over the world.

Krk Island, Croatia

Tourism also plays a part in the economies of this region. There are countless things to see and do. Visitors to the region love to see the well-preserved historic buildings. The castles and churches are marvelous sights. There are palaces to visit, too. In Czechia, Prague is regularly used as a filming location for movies and television. One of the largest film studios in Europe is in Prague. This brings in new people to the country.

Invention of Street Lights

Romania was the first place in Europe to have lighted streets. This happened in the early 1880s. The small town of Timisoara had 731 bulbs strung through town. This innovation led to electric power all over the country.

Proud and Resolute

Given the varied nature of the land and climate, it is hard to speak of eastern Europe as a single region. This is also true of its people. There is a wide range of traditions and beliefs. The region consists of many ethnicities. There are a number of Indigenous groups, too.

In eastern Europe, some people are **skeptical** about their leaders. It is easy to understand their lack of trust based on their history. But the region's people are resilient. Many young people are determined to make a change. Citizens are finding creative ways to engage with their communities.

With each passing year, these countries grow in wealth. The world depends on their hard work and innovation in many ways. This is a region that will continue to grow its economy.

Children participate in a festival in Belgrade, Serbia.

Vilnius Town Hall Square in Lithuania

The cultures of eastern Europe are lively and varied. Many people there take great pride in their heritage. They gladly share their traditions with others. They face challenges with great strength. The proud and resolute nature found in eastern Europeans is strong. It defines that part of the world.

Sharing Traditions

Festivals are a fun way for people to share their traditions with one another. Festivals happen year-round in eastern Europe. In Ukraine, they celebrate the annual harvest festival. This takes place near the end of summer. They give thanks for their crops and walk through fields singing. The festival ends with a big feast.

Map It!

Now that you've learned about eastern Europe, it's time to map it! Grab a partner and a sheet of paper. Choose a country in this unique region, and discover more about it.

1. Which country in eastern Europe are you most curious about? Talk to your partner and choose a country together.

2. Use a poster board or a sheet of paper to sketch a map of your country. Do you notice anything unique about the country's shape and size?

3. What other countries border it? Label those as well.

4. Research online. Look up your country's capital city and at least five other major cities. Label them on your map.

5. Are there nearby oceans or rivers in your selected country? Find the locations of these water sources. Use a blue pen or pencil to outline and label them on your map.

6. What other interesting physical features can you find in your selected country? Look for features such as mountain ranges and natural landmarks. Label each feature on your map.

Kaunas, Lithuania

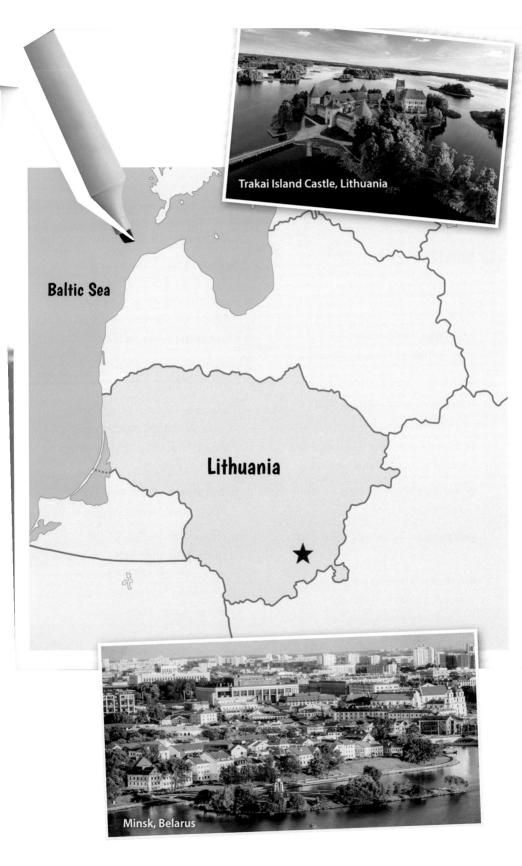

Trakai Island Castle, Lithuania

Baltic Sea

Lithuania

Minsk, Belarus

Glossary

ancestors—people from whom one is descended, such as great-grandparents

coastal—bordering the ocean

corruption—dishonest or illegal behavior especially by people in positions of power

economies—the systems of making, selling, and buying goods and services in particular places

elevation—the height of something above sea level

empires—areas controlled or ruled by a person or group of people

folklore—traditional customs, beliefs, stories, and sayings

generates—brings into existence

Indigenous—from or native to a particular area

latitude—the distance north or south of the equator measured in degrees

nomads—people who move from place to place

oppressed—treated in a cruel or unfair way

resilient—able to recover from difficulties

resolute—determined and unwavering

safeguard—to keep safe

Scandinavia—a region of Northern Europe that includes Norway, Sweden, and Denmark; Finland and Iceland are sometimes included

skeptical—relating to or marked by doubt

Thracian—relating to people who inhabited modern-day Bulgaria, Turkey, and Greece in ancient history

tributaries—rivers that flow into a larger river

turbine—an engine whose central driving shaft is fitted with a series of blades spun around by the pressure of either water, steam, or air

Index

Albania, 5, 7–8, 10

Belarus, 5, 8, 10, 14, 18, 24

Bosnia, 5, 8

Bulgaria, 4–5, 8, 10, 14, 24

Čapek, Josef, 23

Čapek, Karel, 23

communism, 11, 18

Croatia, 5, 8, 25

Czechia, 5, 8, 15, 19, 23–25

Danube River, 8–9

Estonia, 5, 23

Finland, 5, 7, 10, 13

Greece, 4–7, 10

Hungary, 5, 8, 10, 19, 24

Kosovo, 5, 8

Latvia, 5, 23

Lithuania, 5, 16, 27

Moldova, 5, 8, 15, 20, 24

Montenegro, 5, 7

Naumenko, Rita, 21

Nenets, 17

North Macedonia, 5, 8

Poland, 5, 8, 10, 16, 20, 23–24

Romania, 4–5, 7–10, 15, 20, 23–25

Russia, 4–7, 10, 13, 16–17, 21, 24

Sami, 12–13

Scandinavia, 12–13

Serbia, 5, 7–8, 26

Slovakia, 5, 8, 17, 21, 23–24

Slovenia, 5, 8

Ukraine, 5, 10, 17, 21, 24, 27

western Europe, 4, 10

Eger, Hungary

Learn More!

Maia Sandu is Moldova's first female president. She became president in late 2020. She said her greatest priority is to help "people believe again in their country." Research Sandu online to find the answers to these questions. Use your research to create a booklet about her.

- What can you learn about her younger years?
- How did Sandu begin her political career?
- Which organizations has she founded?
- What issues does she care about?